PROFILES IN FASHION

Isaac Mizrahi

PROFILES IN FASHION

Isaac Mizrahi

MORGAN REYNOLDS
PUBLISHING

Greensboro, North Carolina

Profiles In Fashion

JIMMY CHOO

MARC JACOBS

ISAAC MIZRAHI

KATE SPADE

VERA WANG

Profiles In Fashion: Isaac Mizrahi

Library of Congress Cataloging-in-Publication Data

Petrillo, Lisa.
 Isaac Mizrahi / by Lisa Petrillo.
    p. cm. -- (Profiles in fashion)
 Includes bibliographical references and index.
 ISBN 978-1-59935-152-0
1. Mizrahi, Isaac--Juvenile literature. 2. Fashion designers--United States--Biography--Juvenile literature. 3. Fashion designers--New York (State)--New York--Biography--Juvenile literature. I. Title.
 TT505.M595P48 2011
 746.9'2092--dc22
 [B]
                                 2010018312

Printed in the United States of America
First edition

*To Cara, the fashionista whose
great soul inspires us all*

Isaac Mizrahi

Contents

Chapter

1

Different
from the Start

Isaac Mizrahi knew from an early age that he wanted to create his own beautiful world— a dazzling place where everything was filled with great style. Growing up, he loved to go to the ballet and movies with his mother. He especially loved glitter and all things glamorous.

That early exposure to glitz and glamour proved important in the development of Isaac's artistic sensibilities. He would continue to draw inspiration from the theater and movies throughout his life, and eventually he would go on to achieve great success designing for both the stage and the public.

Isaac Mizrahi was born October 14, 1961, in the Brooklyn section of New York City and spent his early childhood in nearby New Jersey. He was the only boy and the baby of his family, with two older sisters. His father, Zeke Mizrahi, was in the clothing manufacturing business. His mother, Sarah, was a homemaker.

Sarah Mizrahi had a good eye for style but did not believe in spending a fortune on high fashion, so she would improve and alter her clothing to make it more personal and stylish. One of Isaac's earliest memories was watching his mother add her own sense of beauty to a pair of high-heeled shoes by gluing imitation daisies on them.

Sarah knew Isaac was different from other boys. At only four years old, he became fascinated with her process of making and altering clothes. He never wanted things like bicycles and baseball mitts. Instead, he wanted to learn how to clip out pieces of fabric and stitch them together into garments. And, Sarah indulged his passions. "To give a child tools, to bring out the child's potential," she said. "That's the most important thing."

Going with his mother to New York City's grand department stores like Bergdorf Goodman and Saks Fifth Avenue was great fun for Isaac. These palace-like stores stood a dozen stories high or more, and covered entire city blocks. Each floor was as big, if not bigger, than a football field and filled with elegance and luxury. And, the emporiums treated customers like royalty.

"She took me shopping everywhere . . . ," Isaac said of his mother. "Her closet was filled with Norells, Balenciagas, Chanels. I'd go to her fittings when Saks had its custom shop. I have all these great visual memories of clothes: a Halston Ultrasuede shirtdress; a Norman Norell ottoman jacket and crystal pleated chiffon pants. Those early years are so important; that's when you form your taste."

Isaac's mother also believed it was important to expose Isaac to the arts. With his mother's strong support, he quickly found an outlet for his passion and creativity.

The family left New Jersey to return to Brooklyn when Isaac was eight. He became seriously ill with spinal meningitis and had to be kept isolated from other children. Meningitis is an infection that inflames the membranes covering the brain and spinal cord. It can cause brain damage and even death. Isaac recovered, and as he recuperated, he comforted himself by eating junk food and watching old movies and TV comedies like *The Dick Van Dyke Show*, starring actress Mary Tyler Moore. Mary Tyler Moore was a stylish woman, a former dancer, and she became one of his favorites.

The Brooklyn Bridge in New York City

Judy Garland was another favorite. Garland, who played Dorothy in *The Wizard of Oz*, had an unhappy life and died from an overdose of drugs. At the family beach club, young Isaac would do impressions of Garland, which horrified his parents, even his otherwise supportive mother.

Around that age he also saw what he would later cite as

one of his greatest influences— an obscure 1961 film called *Back Street*, about a passionate love affair between a fashion designer and a married man. *Back Street* showed him a glamorous world where he wanted to live. For Isaac, even at eight years old, he knew this was it.

While his mother was very supportive, she drew the line with religion. In this one aspect of life, there was little tolerance for deviation from structure and tradition. The family strictly observed the traditional ways of the Jewish religion. That meant honoring the Sabbath, from sundown

A screenshot of Judy Garland in the film *Till the Clouds Roll By*

Fridays to Saturdays, for prayer and reflection. No machinery could be used, including TV. Their food followed kosher laws, including such rules as restricting pork from their diet and forbidding the mixing of dairy foods with meats.

The Mizrahis also sent Isaac to a religious school, a yeshiva, that taught orthodox conservative traditions of the Jewish religion. The teachers were mostly rabbis, who wore long beards and dressed in plain black clothes in the manner of centuries past. What was important in this world was not the external that fascinated young Isaac, but the internal spiritual self. One man determined to do good deeds, he was taught, could change the world.

Strong-willed Isaac rebelled against the strict school rules and was constantly in trouble. He mimicked the severe and serious rabbis. He daydreamed his classroom time away. He horrified his teachers by sketching dress designs in his religious books. What's more, his exuberance and theatrical flair marked him as gay at a time when society did not accept homosexuality openly.

Prejudice against nonconformity was strong. Boys and men were expected to stick to behaviors and interests that were deemed "manly," like sports and business—not the arts. School authorities saw Isaac's refusal to conform as a mental illness and demanded he be sent to a psychiatrist by the age of six. "They thought I was sacrilegious," he later recalled. "They told my parents I was very abnormal."

Jewish religious relics including a shofar, or a ram's horn used during Yom Kippur and Rosh Hashanah; a Torah pointer, a long stick used for pointing to words in the Torah; the Chumash, one of the five books of Moses and part of the Torah; the Tanakh, the canon of the Hebrew Bible; a vessel to wash hands; Shabbot, or Sabbath, candlesticks, and an etrog box, containing the citrus fruit etrog that is used during the holiday Sukkot

Isaac was expelled, and suspended, from the Yeshiva several times. After each expulsion, his mother would put on a plain dress, remove her red nail polish and jewelry, and go there to plead for her son's return. "Once the school took me back, we'd go back home, she'd change her clothes, and we'd go to lunch," he said.

When he was ten, Isaac had been clamoring for a sewing machine, not caring that some considered this an unmanly thing for a boy to want. Even as a child, his drive to create could not be denied. On a summer family vacation, he found an old Singer machine he bought with money he had saved up from babysitting. He set up his own workroom in the family basement and designed clothes for his puppets. He would put on puppet shows for the neighborhood and hire himself out for birthday party entertainment. His ambition now had its first outlet: he became a businessman and an entertainer before he even reached his teenage years.

He grew so skilled at making and designing clothes that by age thirteen, he graduated to designing for people. He designed his own clothes as well as outfits for his mother and her friend, Sarah Haddad. For his mother he made an outfit the color of rust and ivory to complement her dark features. The outfit featured a double-faced skirt, a technique that showed quality workmanship because it was finished on

An antique Singer sewing machine

both the topside and the underside. He completed the ensemble with a matching Shetland wool stole, a wrapped sweater-like garment worn about the shoulders. It was a testament to his design and technical sewing abilities that fashionable women such as his mother and her friends would wear a teenager's design, given their high standards.

"I would tell everyone, 'Look what My Isaac made for me,'" Sarah Mizrahi recalled of his first effort. "The whole neighborhood was talking about that jacket."

His father's attitude toward his only son was to offer encouragement. Isaac received his bar mitzvah at age thirteen, marking in the religious Jewish tradition the passage from childhood to becoming a man. To mark the important occasion, Zeke Mizrahi gave him a pair of professional-level sewing scissors engraved with his name, a symbol of support.

Isaac was miserable at his conservative religious school. But he was lucky enough to find a favorite teacher who understood him. She recognized that Isaac was not mentally ill; he simply had different tastes and sensibilities. She encouraged him to audition for Manhattan's High School of the Performing Arts. It was a free public school, and it was special because it nurtured young artistic talents in a way other schools did not.

It was very competitive to get in to the school, but Isaac won acceptance at age thirteen. His life changed forever. "At Performing Arts, everybody was pregnant, on drugs or discovering whatever their latent sexual tendencies might be. There, artists weren't considered odd. And it was my first exposure to New York city without my parents—culture shock!"

Within one semester he had transformed himself, losing seventy-five pounds so he was no longer a pudgy overprotected "mama's boy." The school became the centerpiece for

Tailoring tools

a Hollywood movie, called *Fame*, and Isaac earned a small role in the popular 1980 film, appearing in an outfit of his own design.

In addition to academics at the High School of the Performing Arts, he took classes in diction, speech, singing, and dancing. He became an accomplished piano player. These skills would all help him in later years. With the school nourishing his artistic soul, he became more confident, and by age fifteen launched his own clothing label, IS New York.

To launch his business, he found financial backing and business connections from his mother's dear friend, Sarah Haddad. But her husband became seriously ill, and she was forced to turn her attention and support away. He learned his first lesson about the struggles and hard reality of sustaining a successful business. His first label closed, but he did not give up. To the contrary, he was just getting started on his quest to redesign the world.

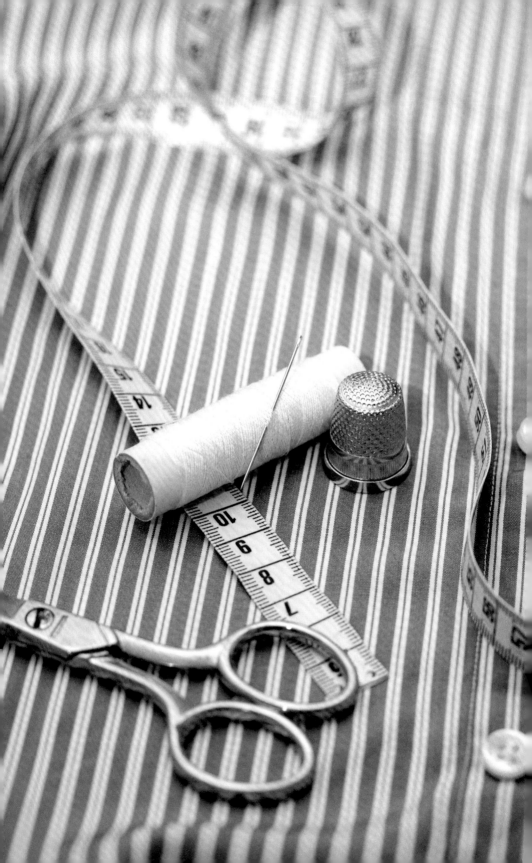

Chapter

2

Learning the Rag Trade

Isaac Mizrahi continued to create designs, and his father showed the sketches to a respected colleague in the clothing manufacturing business. Zeke Mizrahi wanted to see what an unbiased observer would say about Isaac's chances. The businessman told Isaac's father that his son was indeed talented enough to make it in the rag trade, as the fashion industry was called. He encouraged him to send Isaac to the Parsons School for Design. Parsons was one of the best schools of higher education in the arts.

At Parsons in New York City's artsy Greenwich Village section, Mizrahi quickly rose to star student. He won a student design contest before distinguished judges who included Calvin Klein and Donna Karan, a graduate of the school herself. He won for a striped linen pinafore, a sleeveless smock-like garment, paired with a checked dress made out of linen.

He landed a summer job with top clothing designer Perry Ellis. Ellis served as Mizrahi's first real mentor in the fashion industry. After graduation from Parsons, Mizrahi returned

Top: Washington Square
Park in Greenwich Village,
Manhattan

Bottom: MacDougal Street
in Greenwich Village

for full-time work at Perry Ellis. It was a testament to his talent and skill that he landed such a solid job at a major design house fresh out of college. Mizrahi worked long hours, learning all he could about every aspect of the fashion industry.

"He was a poet, a real artist," Mizrahi said of Ellis. "In retrospect I know I took so much and he gave everything — from exposing me to the fabric market, to teaching me not to be too concerned with what the press expects from you."

Tragically in 1983, Ellis became seriously ill with AIDS. In the early 1980s not much was known about how AIDS was caused or spread. It struck hard and fast in the homosexual community, and was greatly feared as a disease. Perry Ellis died in 1986. Around the same time, Mizrahi's father died. In short succession, he lost two of the most important role models in his life.

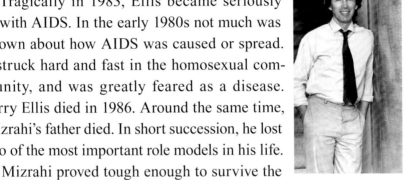

Perry Ellis

Mizrahi proved tough enough to survive the turmoil of the big business of fashion, the financial fragility, and high-stakes feuding. He left Perry Ellis after two years and joined another top name design firm, Calvin Klein. He created one of the company's eye-catching collections, highlighted by streamlined red suits. He credited Klein with teaching him about the business and about tailoring clothes to fit perfectly. He learned important lessons about eliminating, he recalled, the process of trimming back excess fabric to create cleaner lines.

He did not stay long with Klein, though. Brimming with ideas, in June 1987, he rejoined forces with his old financial backer Sarah Haddad-Cheney. Now that he had his own money saved up, they collaborated as partners and started another Isaac Mizrahi company of women's wear. He worked hard, slowly crafting his clothing and delivering the designs himself from the backseat of Cheney's car.

In September 1987 he presented his first fashion show and captured the fashion industry's attention. He convinced influential fashion journalists to come to his show. Those in attendance realized that they had become the first to witness the unveiling of a major new talent. With his attention-getting colors and designs that dazzled with femininity, Mizrahi stood out in a sea of black clothes that so many designers presented and so many women were wearing. Black was considered chic, but Mizrahi's designs proved otherwise. "Color consumes most of my time," he said, "and nourishes me."

The industry praised his fresh approach, saying he combined glamor and elegance with simplicity. He mixed unusual and vivid colors and used bold patterns, including the old-fashioned plaid, a design from centuries past not really considered high fashion. His first line featured sophisticated 1950s-inspired cocktail dresses with their flared skirts and womanly fitted bodices around the ribs and waist. He was a smash, selling to seven major stores in his first season.

Mizrahi's Fashion Influences

Claire McCardell

Born in Frederick, Maryland, in 1905, designer Claire McCardell is best known as the originator of ready-to-wear fashion in America. During the first half of the twentieth century, she helped define what was later known as the American Look. Known for her design innovation, McCardell experimented with unconventional fabrics for various sizes of women. She believed that clothes should be practical, comfortable, and feminine to fit in with the changing lifestyles of American women. During World War II when clothing and fabrics from Europe were unavailable, McCardell prospered by designing clothes that were stylish yet simple and inexpensive. During World War II, McCardell designed the first version of her popover dress, which was a wrap around, unstructured, blue denim dress that was worn over other clothes. McCardell died in 1958 at the age of fifty-three of colon cancer. She influenced many American fashion designers who would follow, including Isaac Mizrahi. A November 1998 *New York Times* article about McCardell noted that "Isaac Mizrahi's collections, including his last one now in the stores, were rich with references to McCardell, like a red satin ballgown with baby carrier, the 90's descendant of that first kitchen popover dress."

Geoffrey Beene

After dropping out of medical school at Tulane University in his home state of Louisiana, Geoffrey Beene moved to New York in 1947 and studied at the Traphagen School of Fashion. He worked at a number of fashion houses in Paris and New York before opening his own company, Geoffrey Beene, Inc., in 1963. His clients included famous actresses such as Faye Dunaway and Glenn Close and the wives of presidents Johnson, Nixon, and Reagan. During the 1970s, Beene was the first American designer to show his lines at the major fashion shows in Europe. He is credited with helping to give American fashion design global credibility. A winner of numerous design awards, Beene was also noted as a mentor to other designers. Several of his apprentices went on to become successful designers, due in part to Beene's help. He died of cancer in 2004.

Halston

He became such a legend that he was able to go by just one name: Halston. He was born Roy Halston Frowick in 1932 in Iowa, at the height of the Great Depression. Halston became famous in the fashion world in the early 1960s as a hat maker for the elite department store chain, Bergdorf Goodman and, famously, for Jacqueline Kennedy, the stylish wife of the glamorous President John F. Kennedy. Jacqueline Kennedy wore one of his hats when her husband was inaugurated in 1961. Halston opened his first shop in Chicago and later relocated to New York. He founded his women's wear label in 1968, thanks in part to his connections with celebrities. *Newsweek* magazine dubbed Halston "the best designer in America" in 1972. In 1973, Halston sold his name to a major corporation. Halston was also known for excessive partying, which included alcohol and drug abuse. He was fired from his own label in the 1980s, and died from complications of AIDS in San Francisco, California, in 1990. His brand name lives on. Today, the Halston fashion collection is created by a team of designers.

Norman Norell

Norman Norell was born Norman David Levinson in Noblesville, Indiana, in 1900. The son of a men's clothing salesman, Norell's childhood dream was to become an artist. At nineteen he went to New York to study art and changed his last name to Norell. He began his professional career as a costume designer, and his simple, stylish clothing was praised for its glamour, timelessness, and high quality. Norell was considered the first American fashion designer to compete successfully with French designers. When he died on October 26, 1972, the *New York Times* ran a story about his life on the front page with the headline: "Made 7th Ave. the Rival of Paris." As the "Dean of American Fashion," Norell was the first to have his name on a dress label, and the first to produce a successful American fragrance, Norell, with a designer name.

Chanel

Gabrielle (Coco) Chanel, was one of the best-known fashion designers of the twentieth century. Although she died in Paris in 1971, the Chanel brand name and design philosophy are still alive. Chanel opened her first shop, selling hats, in Paris in 1909. By 1915 she was well known in the French fashion world. In 1921 she introduced her first perfume, Chanel No. 5, her signature cardigan jacket in 1925, and in 1926, the "little black dress." When World War II began in 1939, Chanel retired and moved into the Hôtel Ritz Paris with her boyfriend, a Nazi officer. When the Germans were defeated, Chanel moved to Switzerland to avoid reprisals for her association with the Nazis. She returned to Paris in 1953 and re-established the Chanel brand. At the time of her death, she was eighty-seven and still working. After Chanel's death, Karl Lagerfeld was hired as the firm's chief designer, and the brand extended its reach into new areas including watches and firearms.

New York City's Grand Department Stores

To a young Isaac Mizrahi, New York City's department stores in the 1960s must have seemed like glittering palaces of all things beautiful. Two of the most glamorous department stores in New York are Bergdorf Goodman and Saks Fifth Avenue. For Mizrahi, these stores were not only an inspiration in his early life, they became important customers from the beginning design career. Bergdorf Goodman caters to a core audience of sophisticated, conservative shoppers but also sells designer collections to satisfy its younger customer with more modern tastes. In 1914, Bergdorf Goodman became the first American clothier to introduce ready-to-wear, making it a destination for American and French fashion. Although it is an icon of luxury retailing, Bergdorf Goodman never successfully expanded beyond New York City. Today it is a subsidiary of the Neiman-Marcus department store chain. Saks Fifth Avenue, founded in 1867, is a luxury American specialty store that has itself become an upscale brand. In the 1920s, the original Saks store merged with another famous New York department store, Gimbles. Saks soon began expanding, surviving the financial turmoil of the Great Depression and World War II to grow to a chain of fifty-three department stories and fifty-five Off 5th discount fashion stores.■

Bergdorf Goodman department store on Fifth Avenue in New York City

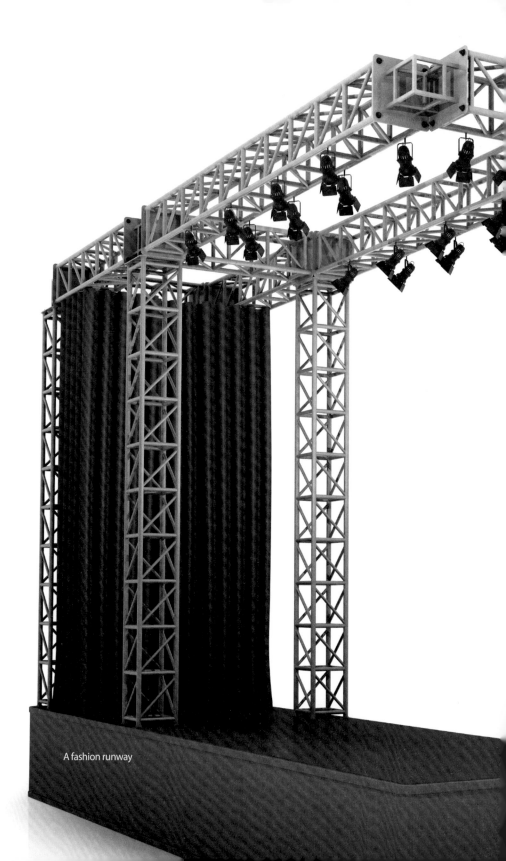

A fashion runway

Chapter
3

Run of the
Runway

C over after cover of fashion magazines featured Isaac
Mizrahi designs in the following years. The influential *Harper's Bazaar* fashion magazine featured
Mizrahi's new coat in its February 1988 issue, which it hailed
as "the newest, grandest after-dark accessory."

Mizrahi had begun to lead the way by mixing influences to
create something new in a world where little else seemed new.
He convinced Manalo Blahnik, the master shoe designer of
high spike heels, to design a Hush Puppy-style shoe. Classic
Hush Puppies are suede comfort shoes, which became very
popular in the 1960s. The Mizrahi twist resulted in a stunning
shoe pepped up in bright Mizrahi colors. Women snapped
them up.

As a businessman and fashion leader, he learned quickly
to use his wit and smarts to endear himself to influential
media and fashion industry leaders. He strived to make himself known as more than the flavor of the month, or some

superficial newcomer. He had no desire to be here today, gone tomorrow.

He talked up the intellectual inspiration for his first collection, which he named after *King Lear*, the classic tragedy by William Shakespeare. His later collections would be inspired

by equally unusual and eclectic subjects, including Old England's King Arthur legends, classical Greek and Roman ruins, and *An Exaltation of Larks*, a book about nouns, phrases, and wording.

He won such positive attention from the industry that in May 1988 he got a chance to meet the legendary beauty and film actress Audrey Hepburn, a style trendsetter for decades. She had starred in such classic films as *Breakfast at Tiffany's* and *My Fair Lady*. The top fashion photographer of the day,

A 1769 painting of Ludwig Devrient as King Lear

Richard Avedon, photographed the elegant Hepburn in Mizrahi's designs.

In 1989, soon after going into business, his clothing design collections earned him a major award from the Council of Fashion Designers of America: the Perry Ellis Award for New Fashion Talent. The following year, Mizrahi followed up that success by winning the Council of Fashion Designers' Designer of the Year Award. He also won best designer of 1990 by the Fashion Footwear Association of New York. Many awards and accolades would follow, year after year.

He made show-stopper outfits but also made sure to appeal to all ranges of his client base by creating the basics, coats, blouses, and handbags as well as evening wear. In the 1980s

Audrey Hepburn

he became crazy about tartan plaid—normally for the more traditional dresser, in places like the British Isles. But Mizrahi turned tartan plaid into evening wear for his 1989 collection—in particular, an off-the-shoulder evening dress.

Mizrahi's signature style is to borrow from various cultures, and to mix old and make it new again. An eye-catching 1982 design featured an ivory-white strapless dress made vibrant with a yellow rose silk screened on the dress, and then accessorized with a matching flower-print scarf at the neckline.

The media loved and promoted him, not just fashion-industry press whose readers were style-conscious professionals in the retail world and garment industry. His appeal was strong enough to draw general newspaper coverage and magazines and TV shows that mainstream America tuned into: *Vogue*, the *New York Times*, *Time*, and *Vanity Fair*. And Isaac always delivered great headlines and powerful photos and video with his intense dark eyes, his imposing six-foot-plus stature, his exotic looks, and his thick dark curly hair. He also delivered flamboyant surprises, like wearing orange toenail polish while being interviewed by serious financial journalists.

He also liked to pop off amusing and offbeat statements like, "It's Giselle meets Fred Flintstone." (Giselle is the star of a beautiful and tragic ballet by the same name, and Fred Flintstone is a modern stone-age cartoon character.)

In 1995 his already colorful designs went pink, and he declared, "Pink is

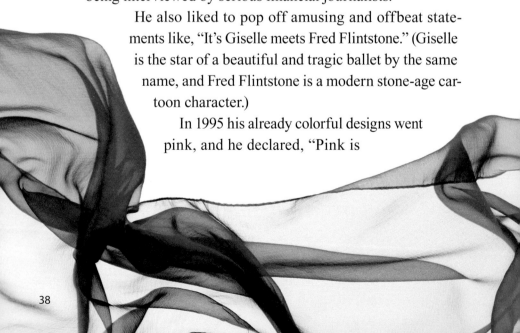

the new neutral. My favorite color of all time is coming into its own and finally the world understands it. What it says is, 'Yes, I'm all woman—and I'm thoroughly in control.'"

Mizrahi seemed to have conquered the world of high fashion. He starred in the elite and exciting world of glamour and gorgeous super models, enjoying the thrill of jetting all over the world. His customers were the wealthy, who could afford to pay more for a single outfit than what most average Americans earn in one year.

Already a fashion star, Mizrahi's stardom then went viral. Douglass Keeve, who was dating Mizrahi at the time, realized what star quality Mizrahi had. He turned him into a super celebrity by documenting Mizrahi as he prepared for his next fashion collection. The resulting 1995 film, *Unzipped*, became a huge hit.

Naomi Campbell

Isaac Mizrahi exposes it all for the camera in *Unzipped*. He cries, he yells, he laughs, he confesses to his mother, and he takes a bubble bath on camera. Though fifteen years old, the film remains so popular it is still widely available in stores, on the Internet, and at libraries. It is considered among the best movies about fashion ever made.

What makes the movie so popular is that the story it tells is timeless: it's about an artist trying to shape and redeem himself. It begins on a bleak and frigid winter morning in Manhattan with Mizrahi. He's exhausted from putting on his big fashion show the day before. It was the culmination of months of work. He walks to a newsstand to buy the leading fashion newspaper and reads the reviews, which trash him and his personal vision expressed in the collection. Viewers see Mizrahi read the bad news and his reaction of feeling like a failure, a very public failure.

Critics say of his last collection, "Was this collection half full or half empty? That was the obvious question . . . " Mizrahi reads the negative review aloud, "What he dubbed a mix was usually a mess. . . . His sense of how a modern woman dresses after 8 p.m. failed him."

He returns to his apartment sitting by the window, smoking, and looking out at the spread out before him and broods. "I hate mediocre things said about me," he says.

The documentary hides little from view. All of Mizrahi's insecurities, his many and varied passions, his manic energy, and his creative process are caught on film and spliced together in an entertaining and logical way. You don't have to know or love fashion to be interested in watching the whirlwind fashion designer Isaac Mizrahi in action.

After the audience sees a vulnerable Mizrahi, he shows us his grit and determination, as he gears up to fight back with an even greater collection the next season. Viewers get to see the entire process of how it's done from design sketches to catwalk. The way it works is, Mizrahi explains, "I get inspired. Somehow. Somewhere."

Mizrahi sees inspiration everywhere and anywhere. Old movies. TV shows. The ballet. He seeks inspiration and

Mary Tyler Moore

guidance from psychics, including an astrologer who reads his fortunes from the stars in the sky. He gets very excited about how through a fortune-telling device called an Ouija board he hears advice to design evening wear. An Ouija is a flat board with letters and symbols some people claim can connect them to spirits that, with the proper setting, can communicate messages.

Bursting with energy and ideas, Mizrahi is always sketching and designing. His worktable sits in the center of his apartment. And then, suddenly, he finds his inspiration for the next collection in an unlikely documentary, *Nanook of the North*, about Eskimos from 1922.

He creates as one of the centerpieces of his new spring line what he calls "The Beast" —a full-length coat in bright orange fuzzy fake fur. The Beast, he says, will be the perfect coat for wealthy New Yorkers to walk their dogs. He muses how great it would be to design fur pants but knows that the press would react with ugly howls. "I guess American women don't want to look like cows," he says with a sigh.

While *Nanook* is the season's inspiration, one of his long-time influences he often refers to is Mary Tyler Moore, and he often sings the theme song to *The Mary Tyler Moore Show* with its signature line, "You're going to make it after all." He explains, "Mary Tyler Moore and Jackie Kennedy (the former First Lady 1960-62), they taught America what style was."

In his own personal wardrobe Mizrahi favors collarless long-sleeved T-shirts with pleated trousers. For business he sports a white dress shirt tailored to fit perfectly with trousers that are generally dark and pleated and finished with a belt.

Viewers watch him interviewing models to hire for the upcoming show, including one with a shaved head and skull tattoos. (She doesn't get the job.)

Promotional poster for the 1922 documentary *Nanook of the North*

President John F. Kennedy and Jacqueline Kennedy in Dallas, Texas

His glamorous world is filled with supermodels breezing through with perfect posture and high cheekbones. His models include Naomi Campbell, Cindy Crawford, and Kate Moss, the most famous names in the fashion business at the time. They were true supermodels, women who made millions of dollars and made themselves household names by being in such demand their images appeared seemingly everywhere, on magazines, in the media, and in ads endorsing products.

Even though so many famous people come through, Mizrahi is clearly the star and the boss. He firmly tells supermodel Campbell that he will not allow her to wear her naval piercing jewelry in his show. She pouts, but he does not bend.

As eye-catching as the supermodels are, the female star of this film is truly his sixty-plus-year-old mother, Sarah Mizrahi. She reveals so much about her son's talent even as a child. She glows as she talks about how he got his start designing clothes for her and her friends.

Mizrahi blushes, claiming his jacket design for her was "a disaster." But she would have none of it, and chides him gently but firmly for trying to minimize her "eye" for style. Clearly she prides herself on her own fashion sense. He acknowledges she was formative for him as he watched her take clothing and alter it to make it more personal and stylish. He talks about how she took a pair of nice high-heeled step-in backless shoes, called mules, that she turned into a fabulous look by applying imitation daisies to them. Mizrahi was fascinated watching her. For her part, his mother clearly knew at that moment that her son was different. Here he was, only four years old, and already paying attention to how fashion was made.

Mizrahi confesses that as a child he would steal pocket change from her purse so he could go to a fabric store. She reacts not with anger but surprise, for she would have given it to him. She has always been supportive and remains that way. "His first show, I was sobbing," she recalls. "I had no idea he was so sophisticated because he was just a kid. I heard someone behind me say, 'Fashion history is being made.'"

One of the great appeals of *Unzipped* is the close relationship between mother and son. It is not forced or sugarcoated. As he gets closer to deadline and the stress piles up, he has long phone conversations with her—even talking to her on the phone while he takes a bubble bath—and she reassures him about his talent, that he is the greatest and just ignore those meanies in the press and the other designers who copy him. "It's one of the worst weeks of my life honestly," he tells her. She soothes him and helps him carry on. At one point the stress seems to be crushing to Mizrahi, and there are thousands of details still needing to be completed. The shoes are late. The fabric knit is too thin and poorly made for his taste. "Everything is frustrating. Every single thing," he says. "Except designing clothes. That's not frustrating. That's really liberating and beautiful."

He recalls some of the risks he's taken in his life. At age seventeen he had saved up some money—he launched his first clothing business at age fifteen—and bought himself a plane ticket to Paris, going all by himself for his first time away from home. He created a special purple leather ensemble to wear on the plane, he recalls.

Now during the filming of *Unzipped*, he is twice that age, thirty-three, and still taking risks reaching for a triumphant comeback.

The film shows his attention to detail that has made all the difference in his career. He was trained in the theater, and it shows.

He explains that he's tired of showing his creations in the same old place, big white tents erected for fashion shows during New York's big Fashion Week, when all the designers show their wares, and buyers and the media cover the leading edge of fashion.

Mizrahi decides this show needs to be different, to give the audience a complete visual experience. Instead of having a curtain separating from view all the frenzied backstage preparation, he insists on a partially see-through screen, a scrim, common in ballet productions where the dancers can be seen moving to indicate a plot sequence. The women are shocked, for they are barely dressed backstage as they change from

outfit to outfit, and at first they protest. Mizrahi loses his temper at their protests.

In the end his idea proves to be genius. By using the scrim to put the production of fashion on display, all its mad-dash energy from backstage poured into the already excited audience. We see models race around having three people help them yank off their thigh-high boots. His risk at doing his show differently pays off.

He lives in a world of excitement and excitable people. They take their fashion very seriously, "It's so major!" gushes Polly Allen Mellen, creative director of *Allure* fashion magazine. "Be careful of makeup; be careful!"

New York skyline at night

The film shows the sometimes silly and excessive world of high fashion. One supermodel throws a jealous fit because she has been assigned flat shoes when the more famous model gets to wear high heels. With just minutes to show time, she accuses Mizrahi of being prejudiced against white women because of his shoe choices. He remains focused on getting his show running smoothly and ignores her.

As the tension builds and deadline approaches, he loses his temper. His closest assistant brings him the newspaper with headlines about a competing fashion designer who some-how—how we are only left to wonder—beat him to a fashion first by showing his own *Nanook*-inspired fashion line dubbed "Eskimo Chic." How could two top designers create haute couture based on a guy named Nanook sixty-five years after the film was made? Was it fake fur espionage? Mizrahi puts his hands over his face and weeps. It seems a strange thing to cry about – someone else getting credit for being inspired by Eskimos first? But his pain is real and moving nonetheless.

Unzipped builds tension as we, like Mizrahi, are invested in this collection we have been watching him build from the start. The big day is here. We follow him, as he walks the long maze of empty hallways of tent flaps to the stage. Then the crowd gathers, cameras flash. The buzz and anticipation is as loud as a waterfall. We see some of the beautiful people acting quite ugly, because they aren't cool enough to be listed on the guest list, and they treat the people keeping them out with haughty contempt, as if they are lower than dirt to dare keep them away.

The music plays, the models sashay in their lovely Mizrahi-designed clothes. The film thus far has been mostly black and white, saving the color for the finished designs. Now in the climax of the film on the runway with the audience filled with the beautiful people, famous actresses and actors all abuzz, the stage explodes with color and beauty—sequined short evening dresses in yellow, pink, and black sashay by, and ballet-style pleated skirts in bright pink with orange and other vibrant color combinations. He has made beauty out of all the chaos in these last months.

The film finally is fully in color, drinking in the marvelous distinct Mizrahi flirty, feminine, and colorful extravaganza. "Insane with color" is what *Women's Wear Daily* will later call it, as the *Daily* praises his newest collection as a success.

"It has to be the most wonderful twenty minutes of a designer's life," he says of the shows.

Afterward the next day in the gray dawn he walks alone across the frigid winter street to the newsstand to buy *Women's Wear Daily*, and reads the review. The press has declared his new collection a triumph. His face is raw, he is exhausted, but he is proud. Off camera someone begs him to sing the Mary Tyler Moore show theme song, "You're going to make it . . ." He politely refuses and silently walks on back to his apartment. The cameraman asks, was it worth it?

"It's always worth it," says Mizrahi shyly looking at the camera as it fades to black.

Mizrahi takes a bow on the runway with his models at
the showing of his 1997 Spring collection in New York.

Chapter

4

The Big Fall

Unzipped won a major prize at the prestigious Sundance Film Festival, and it sealed Mizrahi's fame far beyond the pages of fashion magazines.

Movie audiences loved watching the designer come on-stage from backstage, fearlessly showing himself with all his flaws and flamboyance. Traditionally designers stay behind the curtain. Their names and images remain mysterious and remote. And most people know little of the jet-setting fashion leaders, even though they dictate style—what colors are in, how high the hemlines go, and whether women wear hats or carry straw handbags from season to season.

Unzipped fueled Mizrahi's star power, and he used his high profile to his advantage. When he launched his new line of clothes in February 1996 in New York, the audience was not restricted to the usual collection of the rich and the stylish. Instead, he broadcast his show live via satellite to locations outside the state, something which had not been done before. This was nearly twenty years before cable television and the

Internet made fashion shows and their behind-the-scenes dramas into mainstream television fare with shows like *Project Runway*.

Project Runway

Project Runway began in 2003 as a reality show, mixing real fashion designers and models competing with each other to create the best outfits, often in a limited time. Designs are judged and each week contestants are eliminated, a show that is competitive like the real fashion business but presented in a more entertaining and streamlined format. ■

Soon Mizrahi would show cable TV channels like "E!" how to make a fortune by delivering glamour to regular people, no matter the size of their waistline or bank account. Now that he had the platform of fame, he began using his spotlight to present his philosophy about style, along with selling his stylish clothes. On his label he inserted two pink stars, to remind customers of his motto: "Inside every woman is a star."

Next, Mizrahi made headlines by announcing a deal with three major Asian markets: Japan, Singapore, and Korea. There would be Mizrahi stores as well as Mizrahi-label boutiques of sections of his clothing inside bigger stores. Only the biggest-name labels received such preferential treatment in the retail and fashion industry. Financially it looked like a smart deal, estimated to generate $150 million in retail sales by the year 2000.

In 1997, he seemed on top of the world. He was so talented he could—and did—make fashion out of things like recycled Coke cans (his spring 1994 Collection) and the skin of a salmon (for the Smithsonian).

Osaka Castle in Chuo-ku, Osaka, Japan

He even designed couture for a 10,000-pound elephant named Rosie, to raise awareness and funds for an animal-rights group trying to stop illegal slaughter of elephants for their ivory.

But Mizrahi was flying so high that when he crashed, he crashed hard.

As he rose to super stardom, his clothing sales failed to match. His company had been earning $10 million a year, but how much of that was profit remained in question. In 1998, his biggest investor, Chanel Inc., the American division of the legendary French fashion house, pulled its financial support. His company shut down.

Many critics blamed his collapse on the designer's failure to establish a defined aesthetic or what they took to calling the missing "Mizrahi Look." Such complaints frustrated Mizrahi for he never strove for a "look" frozen in time. To him, style was more personal and changing, the way humans change their minds, tastes, and likes as they grow and learn new things. He never liked strict rules as a child, and as a mature artist and businessman he avoided them. "You know people are always coming up with these formulas, like, 'Before you leave the house, take off one thing.' I mean what's that all about? . . . That's what style is: going with your first choice, giving in to impulse."

Another factor attributed to Mizrahi's fall was his failure to develop lucrative licenses for his designs, or a cheaper collection for high-volume business. "For me, it's bittersweet," he said. "I don't know what

Some of the cast of *Unzipped*. From left: Naomi Campbell, Isaac Mizrahi, and Linda Evangelista

The *New York Times* headquarters in New York City

it says about fashion. I don't know what it says about me. A lot of it is luck."

News that Mizrahi planned to close his business made the front page of the *New York Times*, with its 1 million-plus readers. The headline read,

Mizrahi, Designer Most Likely to Succeed, Doesn't.

Some important fashion leaders stuck by him. Dawn Mello, president of Bergdorf Goodman, said Mizrahi's line was never a top seller but was important nonetheless because it showed the store's support of American designers and aesthetic. "He's a very important representative of

American fashion and we have so much European fashion here at Bergdorf we like to represent American fashion when we can," Mello said. "That's why it's particularly upsetting when we lose a designer collection like this."

"It's very sad," said Liz Tilberis, the editor in chief of *Harper's Bazaar*. "A smile has gone out of the fashion industry. But the saddest part is we are heading toward a kind of mediocrity. I mean commercialism. Of course, we have to have commercial clothes in the stores. But we must have a little madness."

Some critics took the view that women avoided buying Mizrahi because they wanted to be taken seriously in places like Wall Street and felt his clothes too wild, according to the *New York Times*. "Some of the fault for the closing of his company must lay with Mr. Mizrahi. Sometimes his clothing owed more to 1950's television dreamscapes than to women's lives," wrote one critic.

Reflecting on his rise and fall in the fashion industry, Mizrahi said "I never imagined my role as a designer diminishing and my role in film making expanding. It's not what I dreamed of 12 years ago. As an artist, I feel there is something noble about fashion.

"I'm very good at some things," Mizrahi conceded, "but I'm not terribly good at developing a business."

Nevertheless, Mizrahi did not waste time feeling sorry for himself. He kept creating and moving forward. After all, he was in a business that was all about what was hot, au courant, the latest and greatest.

After his backers dropped their funding, Mizrahi said he realized that he had three choices, "One was operating on a shoestring. Another was finding other backers. The third was closing. I thought, 'Move on, darling. Move on.'"

A model steps forward under a shower during Isaac Mizrahi's presentation of his Spring 1998 Collection at the eighth annual "Fire & Ice Ball" in Los Angeles.

Promises, Promises at the Broadway
Theater in New York City

Chapter

5

Conquering New Worlds

O ne of Mizrahi's many ventures outside the fashion design business was a film production company he formed. He was working with the most prestigious director and media mogul of the time, Steven Spielberg, and Spielberg's DreamWorks studio. They worked on a deal to turn into a movie Mizrahi's comic book collection, *Isaac Mizrahi Presents the Adventures of Sandee the Supermodel.*

Sandee is about a beautiful, innocent young woman from the small town of Bountiful, Utah, who is discovered by a top fashion designer. On her way to becoming a world-famous supermodel, Sandee encounters many dangers like any super-hero in the comics. She must battle petty cat fighting from fellow models. She stumbles on drug problems. Her life is threatened by an eating disorder. With Sandee, Mizrahi could also deliver satire criticizing the shallowness of the fashion industry. It also sent an important message to the young, especially young girls, who might damage their health trying to meet the impossible standards the fashion world insisted on setting.

Mizrahi also sent the message that people shouldn't spend themselves into the poorhouse trying to keep up with fashion, and they shouldn't become so obsessed with the latest fads that they wear outfits that don't suit them, making them look foolish. "Fashion slaves" was the slang nickname for such women. Sandee was never made into a movie, but it was still another step toward his goal of trying to teach women to become stylish in a more natural and healthier way.

Mizrahi branched into designing for the theater as well. He became successful creating costumes for plays, dance, TV, and even opera. He designed for shows starring such major dancers as Mikhail Baryshnikov, one of the greatest ballet dancers of the twentieth century. In 2002, Mizrahi received a prestigious theatrical award for his costume designs for a Broadway show of the classic play, *The Women*.

Mikhail Baryshnikov and
actress Leslie Brown in
The Turning Point

Isaac Mizrahi poses
in his design studio
in New York.

While sidelined from fashion, he created and starred in his own New York theatrical production, presenting a song and dance entertainment cabaret called, *Les Mizrahi*. The title was a clever take-off on an enormously popular theatrical production then breaking box office records on Broadway and in London called *Les Miserables*. The musical extravaganza was based on the nineteenth-century classic novel of French characters struggling for redemption and revolution.

In his show, Mizrahi put himself on display singing, and telling stories about the fashion industry. Mizrahi also displayed his design skills during the show, drawing quick sketches and using an old-fashioned sewing machine to create articles of clothing. Though some critics noted that singing was not his strong suit, they called it solid entertainment. And so Mizrahi triumphed by turning himself into a hit in yet another genre of the arts.

Next, Mizrahi turned his attention to cable television. Cable revolutionized entertainment by interconnecting people globally and delivering hundreds of different channels and programming options to viewers.

On cable TV, Mizrahi launched an offbeat talk show, *The Isaac Mizrahi Show*. He attracted a steady stream of celebrity guests from the fashion and entertainment worlds. Mizrahi offered audiences amusing and always different activities, like a series of great afternoon teas with surprising guests. One of his shows featured him taking late-night talk show host Conan O'Brien shopping for ties. On another he taught a gorgeous actress how to do something as old-fashioned and charming as knitting a hat.

Somehow this highly unusual man with his flamboyant ways and rarefied lifestyle connected with the average viewer. His honesty endeared him to viewers—people felt safe that he was not out to hustle them or sell things they didn't need. In fact, he often talked to his audience about NOT shopping or spending a fortune on their wardrobe. He preached quality, not quantity. "For me the whole issue of style isn't so much about money. I believe that most women have too many clothes in their closets, and they don't know what to do with them. You know?"

Rude, Crude, And Unglued

Sometimes Mizrahi has become too unzipped for general audiences. He scandalized television viewers in 2006 on the popular "E!" cable network when he openly gaped down the evening gown of shapely actress Teri Hatcher. And, he grabbed the breast of actress Scarlett Johansson. He questioned actress Hilary Swank about being single, during a time when she was publicly in a painful breakup with husband Chad Lowe. Worse, he asked many celebrities whether they were wearing underwear. ■

Scarlett Johansson

Mizrahi during an interview on *The Tonight Show* with Jay Leno on January 11, 2007

art and expression. He felt good about connecting with people from all walks of life.

Mizrahi continued to draw on his celebrity as well as his training as an actor. He turned up on television and in movies, including as his designer self in the cult-favorite, *Sex & the City*, about fashion-forward single women making their way in the big city, and *Ugly Betty*, about the fashion industry. He showed he was not some superficial airhead by appearing on—and winning—*Celebrity Jeopardy*, the challenging game show. He donated his prize money to the American Society for the Prevention of Cruelty to Animals.

Harry the Beloved Dog

One of Mizrahi's favorite subjects is talking about his dog, Harry, who he adopted from the pound. He considers one of his life's most important milestones was getting Harry, who he declares has made his life complete. "From the moment I met him I knew I loved him madly. It still feels like that," Mizrahi said, "Harry was quite aloof in the shelter, and 'I thought, this is perfect, he doesn't need me.' Then, the minute I got him home, he turned into the neediest thing in the world. Two weeks in, I thought: 'I'm trapped.' But then I realized you get all of this affection by giving up a tiny bit of freedom. That's the price of love, darling. And that was what was missing from my life: Love without borders." ∎

Mizrahi poses with his dog, Harry, before the start of the Target pet fashion show in February 2005, in New York.

Isaac Mizrahi is
applauded following
his Fall 2004 fashion
show in New York.

Chapter

6

Returning to the Fold

As exciting and rewarding as his life was discovering new fields to conquer, Mizrahi couldn't stay away from the fashion world. In 2003 he announced his return to his first love, fashion, in a spectacular way.

He launched two new ventures appealing to completely different audiences at the same time. He launched a line for his high-end fashionistas, delivering custom-made designs for those willing to spend thousands on a single outfit. For this venture, he planned to operate through the upscale department store Bergdorf Goodman with prices starting at about $5,000. At the same time he would design clothes for the international discounting giant retailer Target, with prices starting at about ten dollars.

While many questioned if this new model would work— Was it possible to create great style with such low cost? Could Mizrahi make fashion populist?—Mizrahi proved it was indeed possible. His Target deal proved so fabulously successful he branched from apparel and accessories to bedding,

SuperTarget in Roseville, Minnesota

pet products, household products, and even bridal dresses. He tripled sales volume over five years, by some estimates.

And Mizrahi, who hates to travel, visited the Iowa State Fair to show midwesterners all about Mizrahi style, using his Target line as a foundation. He triumphed in the heartland of America. He appeared on the popular daytime talk show *The Oprah Winfrey Show*, and surprised some of her audience members by giving them makeovers based on his low-cost fashions. His appearance on Winfrey's show, with its millions of viewers, helped Mizrahi cement his credibility as an artist who can design for the wealthy and the working class.

A year after launching his Target line, he really emphasized his philosophy by throwing a big party-style fashion show to demonstrate how to combine high-end fashion with low-end clothing. Mizrahi demonstrated that what matters is the design, not the label underneath the outfit and the status that it accords those who wear the clothes. He deliberately mixed couture designer pieces with his budget clothing on models, calling it the High-Low Show.

One High-Low model wore a denim coat over a blue-lace petticoat. Even some fashion reporters declared they couldn't tell the price difference between the two pieces from afar. Another model wore a black taffeta cocktail dress accessorized with white elbow-length gloves and black flat heels. "To die for!" one critic wrote.

While Mizrahi's discount Target line had made his name even more widely known, he was savvy enough not to abandon the world of high fashion. He continued to design couture but on a limited scale. Now he was able to design without having to worry about managing every aspect of a full-fledged design business complete with fashion shows. Running his

A Bergdorf Goodman window display

own fashion house with all its attendant details had become, as he said, a "drag."

In 2008 Mizrahi became increasingly political. He was an early endorser of then-Senator Barack Obama, and lent his celebrity to the cause designing tote bags—with their fashion-conscious logo, Runway to Change—to raise money and awareness of the future president's message of hope and inclusiveness. He also launched his own extensive Web site that featured such innovations as a Web-video-series, WatchIsaac.com.

And he also launched an Internet site, www.Isaacmizrahiny.com, which is chock full of the designer's unique perspective on a wide range of his many passions: psychics, with whom he regularly consults; his hometown baseball team, the New York Yankees; crossword puzzles; Weight Watchers, which he credits with helping him lose pounds after he quit smoking in 2003, and cooking.

Mizrahi continues his evangelizing about style, still trying to beautify the world, every chance he gets. He even wrote a coffee table-sized hardback book on style. The book features twelve "regular" women who he chose to give complete makeovers.

Barack Obama gives his acceptance speech in Denver, Colorado, after securing the Democratic nomination for president.

Mizrahi in Your Closet

How does a person get style? The answer, according to Isaac Mizrahi, is inspiration. And, he offers a how-to guide in his 225-page book *How to Have Style*.

Mizrahi chose twelve ordinary women of varied ages, lifestyles, body types, races, and backgrounds to make over for his book. His aim: is to teach the building blocks of how to find style. "I have to say something, girls," Mizrahi begins. "Before you can think about having style, you have to learn to look in the mirror and like what you see. Too many women are taught to hate the way they look and are encouraged to change everything about themselves from their lips to their bust sizes."

Throughout the book, Mizrahi repeats his mantra that what matters most is the quality of one's garments, not the quantity. He advises readers to shop a lot, but don't buy: Go places you might never shop and try on clothes you normally would never touch. See new possibilities, in new shapes and colors and styles. Think like an art collector, he further advises. Learn the difference between impulse buying and thoughtful collecting. Instead of wasting money

Mizrahi in his New York studio

A modern businesswoman in a sleek, fitted pinstriped jacket

buying ten cheap shirts, it's better to have one classic jacket that can last for a decade.

Other tips: dress for the occasion. Don't just grab favorite clothes and skip out the door. Be thoughtful. When one of the women featured in the book told him she dresses for herself and her own comfort, except when she's trying to impress someone, he responded. "Sometimes? No, when getting dressed, think about the community you live in. Ask yourself who you are and what/who you are dressing for. How should you look in a particular situation? What will it take that day to make yourself look and feel great?"

On the issue of fit, Mizrahi says badly fitting clothes give a person a careless look, instead of a put-together style. He recommends buying fewer clothes, but spending a little bit more to get clothes to fit by taking them to a tailor or a seamstress, or learn to sew.

Use eBay, but educate yourself first is another Mizrahi recommendation. For one makeover subject, he bought a classic skirt off of the Internet market-place site. But first he advises shoppers to check out high-end stores to get to know designer labels and how those labels fit on you, since sizes vary by the designer. Then when you know your size, you can search on eBay by label or designer, instead of by cate-gory. Searching by category, say for a blouse size eight, can produce thousands of choices.

Mizrahi also suggests women get a small cork bulletin board and fill it with images that inspire—colors they love, images they are drawn to, like ones in movies they watch over and over—and then scatter them across the board randomly.

Another style tip: Shop the boys' department. Garments generally are lower in cost, especially jackets and other basics. The sizing goes all the way to size twenty. And for an instant spa: soak chamomile tea bags in ice water, lie down and place the bags over your closed eyes and rest for five minutes. ■

Among his other ventures in 2009 was a television series on the Bravo cable network called *The Fashion Show.* It was a mix of real fashion shows but with a reality show twist, and amusing challenges and limitations. And, of course, Mizrahi's fashion advice. He also opened a shop in New York City show-casing his ready-to-wear, accessory, and couture collections. While none of these were rock-bottom budget Mizrahi designs like the Target line, he designed the clothes to reach a larger variety of pocketbooks, not just those who can afford to pay thousands for outfits.

After five years designing for Target, Mizrahi left the retailer to take on a new challenge. He launched his own "life-style" collection of household items from dresses to cheese-cakes and women's wear on the premiere cable TV home-shop-ping network, QVC. News of Mizrahi's switch to QVC made it to the press, including in pages of the *Wall Street Journal*:

> The resurgence of Mr. Mizrahi, a designer known as much for his charisma as his clothing, is tied to the many changes sweeping the fashion industry. With cost-conscious conglomerates increasingly in control, many designers are searching for ways to broaden their sales beyond the high-fashion customer. At the same time the growth of collaborations with mid-Ameri-can retailers, the rise of cable television, the birth of reality television and the Internet have created a surge of opportunities—opportunities that happen to suit Mr. Mizrahi's persona. Mr. Mizrahi often says he's adapted to the times, but it's also true that the times adapted to suit him.

Since the 1980s, Isaac Mizrahi has earned fame and fortune, designing everything from high-priced evening gowns to dog food bowls. His artistic achievements have reached even the White House, where he's designed for First Lady Michelle Obama. And though he's won many awards and has a solid reputation in the fashion industry, Mizrahi continually challenges and reinvents himself. "I ask myself when I design every collection, 'What will change style forever?'"

Mizrahi's firm belief that anyone can be stylish, even if strapped for cash, has endeared him to generations of followers. "One thing that you can do no matter who you are or what you look like: You can actually get passionate instead of remaining cool or instead of trying to look like everybody else. You can—you must—immerse yourself passionately in who you are if you want to have style."

Isaac Mizrahi

Timeline

1961 Born October 14 in the New York City borough of Brooklyn to clothing manufacturer Zeke Mizrahi and fashionable housewife Sarah.

1968 Attends a yeshiva, or a traditional Jewish school.

1970 Launches his first "business," holding puppet shows with puppets in outfits he designs.

1972 Buys a vintage sewing machine with money earned by babysitting.

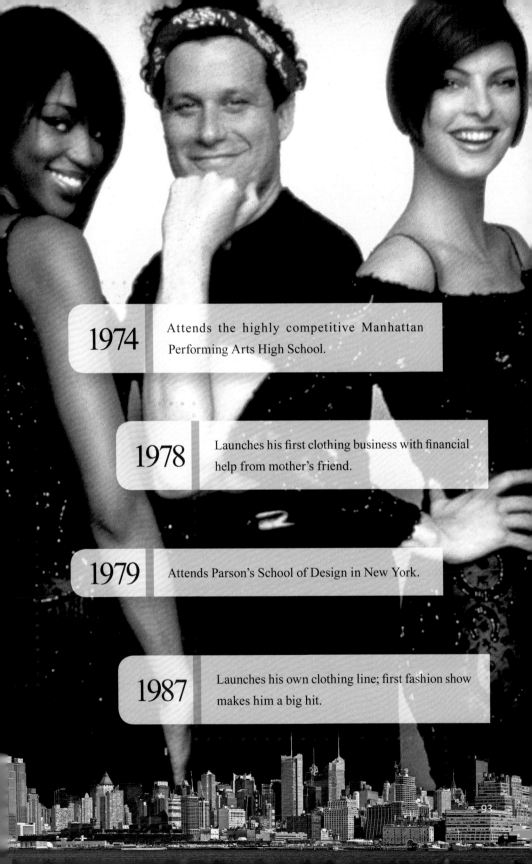

1974 Attends the highly competitive Manhattan Performing Arts High School.

1978 Launches his first clothing business with financial help from mother's friend.

1979 Attends Parson's School of Design in New York.

1987 Launches his own clothing line; first fashion show makes him a big hit.

1989 Wins major fashion-industry award and captures attention of fashion leaders.

1991 Branches into designing for the theater; designs costumes for legendary dancer Mikhail Baryshnikov.

1992 Chosen as one of the top designers for the one hundredth anniversary of *Vogue*; nominated for an Emmy Award for designs for a TV show.

1995 Stars in *Unzipped*.

1998 Shuts down business after his biggest financial investor pulls support; branches into other ventures.

2001 Becomes a hit as a cable TV talk show host.

2002 Tries his luck as an entertainer, appearing in popular TV show *Sex and the City*, and performing at Manhattan nightspot.

2003 Announces partnership with discounter Target to design high-style for low-cost clothing, revolutionizing the industry.

2007 Returns to couture fashion shows with a fall collection; launches into furniture design and continues theatrical productions.

2008 Returns to menswear design; unveils Web site plugging his designs; publishes a book on style; campaigns for Barack Obama.

2009 Debuts a new reality fashion competition show on cable TV.

Sources

Chapter One | Different from the Start

p. 12, "To give a child tools . . . " Mary Rourke, "So Young, So Restless," *Los Angeles Times*, February 2, 1992.

p. 12-13 "She took me shopping everywhere . . ." Bridget Foley, "Isaac Mizrahi the Talk of Seventh Avenue," *Women's Wear Daily*, May 5, 1988.

p. 17, "They thought . . ." Ibid

p. 17, "Once the school . . ." Ibid.

p. 19, "I would tell everyone . . ." Isaac Mizrahi, Sandra Bernhard, Robert Best, Natane Boudreau, and Carla Bruni, *Unzipped,* DVD, directed by Douglas Keeve (Miramax, 1995).

p. 19, "At Performing Arts . . ." Foley, "Isaac Mizrahi the Talk of Seventh Avenue."

Chapter Two | Learning the Rag Trade

p. 25, "He was a poet . . . " Bridget Foley, "Isaac Mizrahi the Talk of Seventh Avenue," *Women's Wear Daily*, May 5, 1988.

p. 26, "Color consumes most . . ." Anne Bratskeir, "Mizrahi Loves Company, With his new cabaret act, Isaac is back where he wants to be - front and center," *Newsday,* October 19, 2000.

Chapter Three | **Run of the Runway**

p. 38,   "It's Giselle meets . . ." Esther Pan, "Mizrahi's Final Bow," *Newsweek*, October 12, 1998.

p. 38-39, "Pink is the new . . ." Isaac Mizrahi, isaacmizrahiny. com, June 1995, http://www.isaacmizrahiny.com/about/timeline/contents/153/june_1995_-_pink.

p. 40,   "I hate mediocre . . ." Mizrahi, *Unzipped*.

p. 40,   "I get inspired . . ." Ibid.

p. 43,   "I guess American . . . Ibid.

p. 47,   "His first show . . ." Ibid.

p. 47,   "It's one of . . ." Ibid.

p. 47,   "Everything is frustrating . . ." Ibid.

p. 49,   "It's so major . . ." Ibid.

p. 51,   "It has to be . . . " Ibid.

p. 51,   "It's always . . ." Ibid.

Chapter Four | **The Big Fall**

p. 59,   "You know people . . ." Ruth Ferla, "Envying Roisterous Lives," *New York Times*, November 30, 1997.

p. 59,   "For me, . . ." Constance White, "Mizrahi, Designer Most Likely to Succeed, Doesn't," *New York Times*, October 2, 1998.

p. 61-62, "He's a very important . . ." Ibid.

p. 62,   "It's very sad . . ." Ibid.

p. 62,   "Some of the fault . . ." Ibid.

p. 62,   "I never imagined . . ." White, "Mizrahi, Designer Most Likely to Succeed, Doesn't."

p. 62,   "I'm very good . . ." "Down, Not Out," *People Weekly*, October 19, 1998.

p. 62-63, "One was operating . . ." Ibid.

Chapter Five | **Conquering New Worlds**

Chapter Six | **Returning to the Fold**

p. 84, "I have to say . . ." Mizrahi, *How to Have Style*

p. 87, "Sometimes? No . . ." Mizrahi, *How to Have Style*.

p. 89, "The resurgence . . ." Rachel Dodes, "Isaac Mizrahi Meets QVC," *Wall Street Journal*, July 24, 2009.

p. 90, "I ask myself . . ." Rourke, "So Young, So Restless."

p. 90, "One thing that . . ."Andrew Macfarlane, "Isaac Mizrahi," *Esquire*, March 1, 2000.

Bibliography

Adato, Allison, and Fannie Weinstein. "A Second Act."
   People, August 18, 2003.

Agins, Teri. "Style & Substance: The Lessons of Isaac;
   What Mr. Mizrahi Learned Moving From Class
   to Mass; Battle of the Hot Pink Blazer." *Wall Street
   Journal*, February 7, 2005.

Bratskeir, Anne. "Mizrahi Loves Company, With his new
   cabaret act, Isaac is back where he wants to be -
   front and center." *Newsday*, October 19, 2000.

Dodes, Rachel. "Isaac Mizrahi Meets QVC." *Wall Street
   Journal*, July 24, 2009.

Foley, Bridget. "Isaac Mizrahi the Talk of Seventh Avenue."
   Women's Wear Daily, May 5, 1988.

Hansen, Liane. "Holiday Style on a Budget," Weekend
   Edition, National Public Radio (transcript),
   December 28, 2008. http://www.npr.org/templates/
   story/story.php?storyId=98766612.

Hutton, Lauren. "*Unzipped.*" *Entertainment Weekly*,
   March 8, 1996.

Ingrassia, Michele. "Mizrahi 'Unzipped.'" *Newsweek*,
   July 24, 1995.

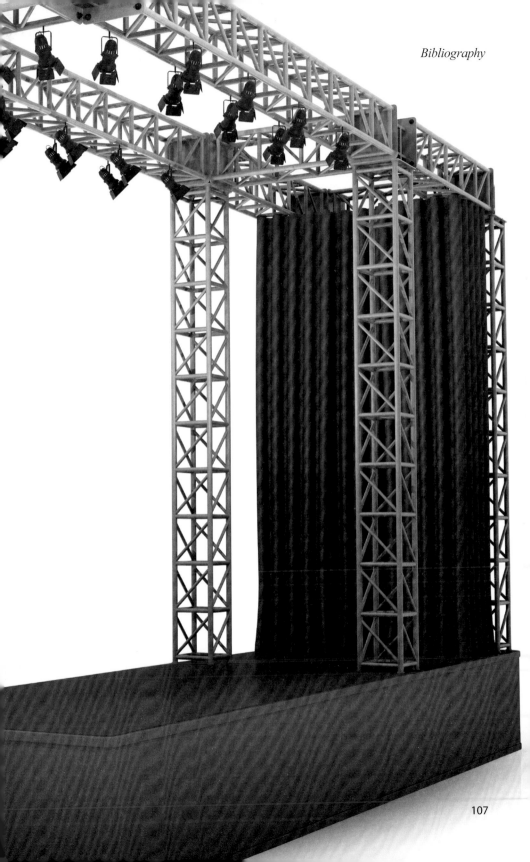

Bibliography (cont.)

Isherwood, Charles. " Les Mizrahi." *Variety,*
    October 30, 2000.

Johnson, Philip D. "The crown prince is back." Lucire.com,
    August 26-29, 2004.
    http://lucire.com/2003/fall2004/0719fe0.shtml.

La Ferla, Ruth. "Envying Roisterous Lives." *New York
    Times*, November 30, 1997.

Mizrahi, Isaac. *How to Have Style*. New York, Gotham
    Books, October 2008.

Pan, Esther. "Mizrahi's Final Bow." *Newsweek,*
    October 12, 1998.

Poniewozik, James. "Reality TV That's a Cut Above." *Time,*
    July 9, 2006.

Rourke, Mary. "So Young, So Restless." *Los Angeles Times*,
    February 2, 1992.

White, Constance. "Mizrahi, Designer Most Likely to
    Succeed, Doesn't." *New York Times*,
    October 2, 1998.

Wilson, Eric, and Michael Barbaro. "Isaac Mizrahi Leaves
    Target to Revamp Liz Claiborne." *New York Times*,
    January 16, 2008.

Yee, Amy. "Target Hopes to Turn Heads off the Catwalk."
    Financial Times, October 21, 2003.

Web sites

http://www.isaacmizrahiny.com
The official Web site of Isaac Mizrahi

http://www.style.com
The Web site of the online magazine, Style.com, which is
part of Conde Nast publications

http://www.wwd.com
The Web site of the newspaper *Women's Wear Daily*

Book cover and interior design by Derrick Carroll.

Index

Photo Credits

8: AP Photo/Peter Kramer,File

10: Used under license from iStockphoto.com

12: Used under license from iStockphoto.com

14: Courtesy of Jleon

16: Private Collection

17: Courtesy of Gilabrand

18: Used under license from iStockphoto.com

20: Used under license from iStockphoto.com

22: Used under license from iStockphoto.com

24 top: Private Collection

24 bottom: Courtesy of GK tramrunner229

25: Private Collection

26: Used under license from iStockphoto.com

32: Courtesy of Christopher Peterson

34: Used under license from iStockphoto.com

36: Private Collection

37: AP Photo

38: Used under license from iStockphoto.com

39: Courtesy of Jgro888

41: Used under license from iStockphoto.com

42: AP Photo/Lennox McLendon

44: Private Collection

45: Courtesy of the U.S. Government

48: Courtesy of David Iliff

52: AP Photo/Bebeto Matthews, file

55: Used under license from Shutterstock.com

56: Courtesy of 663highland

58: Moviestore collection Ltd / Alamy

60: Courtesy of Haxorjoe

63: AP Photo/Michael Caulfield

64: Private Collection

67: Photos 12 / Alamy

68: AP Photo/Jim Cooper

71: Courtesy of the U.S. Government

72: Paul Drinkwater/NBCU Photo Bank via AP Images

74: Used under license from iStockphoto.com

75: AP Photo/Diane Bondareff

76: AP Photo/Louis Lanzano

78: Courtesy of Bobak Ha'Eri

80: Courtesy of David Shankbone

82: Courtesy of David Shankbone

83: AP Images

85: AP Photo/Jim Cooper

86: Used under license from iStockphoto.com

88: Used under license from iStockphoto.com

91: AP Photo/Peter Kramer,File

93: Moviestore collection Ltd / Alamy

95: AP Photo/Jim Cooper

96: AP Photo/Jim Cooper

98: Courtesy of Jleon

100: Courtesy of David Iliff

102: Courtesy of Haxorjoe

104: Courtesy 663highland

107: Used under license from iStockphoto.com